Electric Smoker Cookbook

Many Beginner Smoking Recipes for Your Electric Smoker

Table of Contents

Introduction

Your backyard guide for flawless smoking is finally here! The Beginner Smoking Recipes Cookbook has 30 classic recipes in answer to your call.

Sizzling sides, succulent meats with good smoking flavor, you don't have to be a professional chef to barbecue like one. This book is also for the outdoor cook who wants to up the heat and brings more zest to their grilling skills.

Beginner Smoking Recipes Cookbook equips you to master the art of wood pellet smoking.

This cookbook instructs you how to use your wood pellet grill properly, also, advice on how to get the complete smoke flavor for each cut of meat. With 30 totally delicious recipes for modern and classic favorites, Beginner Smoking Recipes Cookbook is your perfect choice of recipes for everyday grilling and mouthwatering barbecue for all to enjoy.

Pork Tenderloin

You will love this easy method of preparing pork tenderloin. Crispy on the outside and juicy on the inside.

Time: 40 Minutes

Serves: 4

Ingredients:

- Pork tenderloins – 2 ½ pound
- Oil – 1 tablespoon
- Italian seasoning – 2 teaspoons

- Fresh lime, lemon or orange juice – 3 tablespoons
- Chili powder - 1 teaspoon
- Cumin – 1 teaspoon
- Black pepper – ¼ teaspoon
- Italian seasoning – 2 teaspoons
- Smoked paprika – 1 teaspoon

Directions:

1. Get the smoker preheated to 400 deg. F. Pierce the tenderloins using a fork all through then rub oil all over the meat.

2. Whisk the Italian seasoning together with cumin, garlic powder, chili powder, salt, smoked paprika, and black pepper.

3. Sprinkle the mixture over tenderloins as you pat over the surface of the meat then place on all the sides. Place the tenderloins into the smoker then drizzle with lime or lemon juice over the top.

4. Let it bake for 35 minutes or until the outside becomes crispy and brown and the centers are cooked all through to the desired texture.

5. Spoon in the juices over the meat then allow to rest over a cutting board for about 5 minutes. You can then slice into about 1-inch pieces.

6. Spoon the remaining juices over the pan then garnish with some fresh chopped cilantro as desired.

7. Serve and enjoy.

Smoked Pork Shoulder

This recipe uses a simple but easy spice rub. All you need is a few pantry ingredients and a smoker to give you a mouth-watering taste.

Time: 6 Hours 10 Minutes

Serves: 8

Ingredients:

- Boneless pork shoulder – 4 lbs.

Dry Rub:

- Dark brown sugar packed – 2 tablespoons
- Dark chili powder – 1 tablespoon
- Paprika – 1/8 cup
- Dried oregano – ½ tablespoon
- Cumin – 1 tablespoon
- Kosher salt – 2 tablespoons
- Granulated sugar – 1/2tablespoon
- Celery seeds – ½ tablespoon
- Ground black pepper – ½ tablespoon

Directions:

1. Mix all the ingredients for dry rub into a bowl or in a shaker.

2. Trim excess fat off the pork shoulder then rub some liberal amount of the mixed dry rub all over the pork. Save some rub for later use.

3. Cover the pork shoulder then refrigerate overnight.

4. Follow smoker's instructions as you bring the temperature up to 250 deg. F. Place water filled aluminum drip beneath the grates to catch the drippings.

5. Place pork shoulder over the grate and right above the drip pan once the smoker begins to produce smoke.

6. Smoke the beef shoulder for about 1 hour 30 minutes for each pound of pork or until the internal temperature gets to 205 deg. F. Keep monitoring the temperature continuously using a probe thermometer.

7. Remove pork shoulder from the smoker once ready then wrap it with aluminum and allow to rest for about 1 hour.

8. Use a large fork to shred the pork as you pull the strands across for a maintained texture.

Perfect Smoked Pork

Perfect for feeding large crowds. This simple recipe is the most foolproof and versatile slow and low smoked dish you might ever prepare but quite tasty!

Time: 6 Hours 15 Minutes

Serves: 8

Ingredients:

- Boston butt – 8lb
- Garlic cloves – 6
- Fresh oregano – ½ teaspoon
- Fresh thyme – ½ teaspoon
- Large fresh basil leaves – 8
- Chopped Italian Parsley – ¼ cup
- Light brown sugar – 2 tablespoons
- Olive oil – ½ cup

Directions:

1. In a food processor combine all the ingredients apart from brown sugar and pork then grind until it forms a thick green liquid.

2. Rub the mixture over the roast then sprinkle with sugar and use a heavy-duty foil to wrap it up.

3. Place it into a refrigerator and allow it to stay for about 4 hours or even overnight. Soak about 2 chunks of hickory into water then light about 40 coals.

4. Once the coals are well covered with grey ash push them to one side then place the soaked hickory chunks over the coals.

5. Replace the grate then foil wrapped roast and add one cup of water. Place the roast over the cool side of the grill then cover the grill with the holes right over the meat.

6. Turn the roast to 180 deg. F after every one hour. Add some more wood and coal after two hours then smoke the pork for about 6 hours or until the internal temperature reaches 170 deg. F.

7. If the meat is getting too brown, you can add another layer of foil sheet and the temperature within the grill should be 275 deg. F.

8. Once ready remove from the grill then cover with foil and allow to stay for about 20 minutes.

9. Serve with your preferred barbecue sauce and brush some on the roast then allow to stay for 10 minutes.

10. Serve and enjoy

Roasted Rack of Lamb

A delicious centerpiece for an elegant holiday dinner without much fussiness in having it prepared.

Time: 1 Hour 10 Minutes

Serves: 4

Ingredients:

- Fresh breadcrumbs – ½ cup
- Chopped fresh rosemary – 2 tablespoons
- Minced garlic – 2 tablespoons
- Salt – 1 teaspoon
- Trimmed and frenched rack lamb – 1 lb. (7-bone)

- Black pepper – 1 teaspoon
- Olive oil – 2 tablespoons
- Dijon mustard – 1 tablespoon

Directions:

1. Get the smoker preheated to 450 deg. F and move the rack towards the center position.

2. In a bowl mix together garlic, breadcrumbs, rosemary salt and pepper. Toss olive oil to moisten the mixture up then set it aside.

3. Season the lamb as well all over with salt and pepper.

4. Sear the lamb with mustard then roll the bread crumb mixture over the lamb until well coated.

5. Cover the ends with foil to prevent the bones from charring.

6. Arrange the lamb in the skillet then roast in a preheated smoker for about 50 minutes or until the desired doneness is attained.

7. Once the roast is ready, allow it to rest for about 7 minutes before carving then serve and enjoy.

Easy Smoked Vegetables

This simple smoked vegetable recipe is the perfect, easy and quick dish for your smoker.

Time: 1 Hour

Serves: 4

Ingredients:

- Red onion peeled and quartered - 1
- Seeded and sliced red pepper – 1
- Yellow sliced summer squash – 1

- Balsamic vinegar – 2 tablespoons

- Black pepper – ½ teaspoon

- Sea salt – 1 teaspoon

- Olive oil – 2 tablespoons

- Sliced zucchini – 2

- Minced cloves garlic – 6

Directions:

1. Place all the ingredients into a bowl then mix.

2. Get pellet grill preheated to 350 deg. F.

3. Place the vegetables in the grill then cook for about 45 minutes or until the vegetables are cooked through and caramelized.

4. Remove from the grill once ready then serve warm.

Apple Wood Smoked Chicken

This melt-in-your-mouth smoked chicken will wow your taste-buds.

Time: 2 Hours 30 Minutes

Serves: 2

Ingredients:

- Whole chicken halved- 1
- Garlic powder – 1 teaspoon
- Paprika – 1 teaspoon

- Red pepper flakes crushed – 1 teaspoon
- Garlic salt – 1 teaspoon
- Salt – 1 teaspoon
- Cayenne pepper – ¼ teaspoon
- Dried thyme – ½ teaspoon
- Dried oregano – ½ teaspoon
- Brown sugar – 2 tablespoons
- Black pepper – 1 teaspoon
- Apple wood chips to be used for smoking

Directions:

1. In a bowl combine all the ingredients then rub the seasoning mixture all over the chicken halves. Cover the chicken with some plastic wrap then refrigerate for about 1 hour.

2. In a smoking tray place the wood chips then place chicken over the hot grill with the meat side facing down. Grill the chicken for 1 hour 20 minutes and cover to keep off the smoke.

3. Once it has cooked for 30 minutes, turn the chicken and cook until the juices near the bone begins to run clear.

4. Allow to cool for a few minutes then serve and enjoy.

Easy Smoked Chicken

This smoked chicken recipe is very simple. It has a beautiful smokey flavor and it produces succulent breast meat.

Time: 4 Hours 20 Minutes

Serves: 8

Ingredients:

- Whole chicken – 1 (6 pounds)
- Cold water 8 cups

- Morton kosher salt – ¼ cup

Directions:

1. In a saucepan bring a cup of water to boil over a stovetop. Add kosher salt 2 tablespoons to boil then stir well until dissolved. Add the remaining 7 cups of water, then place the whole chicken into a freezer zip top bag and place in a bowl.

2. Transfer salted water into the bag with chicken then zip the bag and seal.

3. Place the bowl that has the chicken into the refrigerator and allow to chill for between 2 – 8 hours.

4. Remove chicken from the refrigerator then discard the salty water and rinse it. Place the chicken over a baking sheet then pat to dry.

5. Use homemade barbecue chicken rub to rub the inside and outside of chicken. Allow the chicken to stay as you prepare the smoker and let the smoking setting be around 160 deg. F.

6. Transfer chicken from the baking sheet then place it over the smoker. Smoke it over 3 hours then increase the

temperature to about 225 deg. F. Continue with the cooking until the inserted thermometer reads 165 deg. F.

7. Remove chicken from the smoker then allow it to rest from 20 minutes. Slice and enjoy.

Smoked Chicken Wings

These smoked dry-rubbed chicken wings are grilled until brown and crispy but also coated with a buttery hot sauce.

Time: 1 Hour 23 Minutes

Serves: 8

Ingredients:

- Chicken wings – 3 pounds

Dry Rub:

- Ground black pepper – 1 ½ teaspoons
- Kosher salt – 1 tablespoon
- Cajun seasoning – 1 ½ teaspoons

Sauce:

- Butter – ½ cup
- Worcestershire sauce – ½ teaspoon
- White vinegar - 1 ½ tablespoons
- Garlic powder – 1/8 teaspoon
- Salt to taste
- Hot pepper sauce – 2/3 cup

Directions:

1. Get the smoker heated to 225 deg. F as per the manufacturer's instructions.

2. In a small bowl mix together Cajun seasoning, pepper and salt into a dry rub then sprinkle the mixture over the kitchen wings.

3. Place the chicken wings over the smoker and cook for 1 ¼ hours. In a saucepan, combine vinegar, butter, hot pepper

sauce, Worcestershire sauce, salt and garlic powder. Place the saucepan over low heat then cook and continue to stir until the butter is well melted and the sauce becomes smooth.

4. Remove the sauce from heat once ready then set aside.

5. Get an outdoor grill preheated and oil the grate lightly. Transfer the smoked wings into a bowl then stir in ½ of the sauce until the wings are well coated.

6. Grill the coated wings for about 5 minutes on each side or until browned lightly crispy.

7. Transfer to a bowl then stir in the rest of the sauce until the wings are evenly coated.

8. Serve immediately and enjoy.

Honey Smoked Turkey

Bring your turkey to a higher level with this delicious recipe which leaves your turkey incredibly moist.

Time:3 Hours 23 Minutes

Serves: 8

Ingredients:

- Whole turkey – 12 pounds
- Fresh sage chopped – 2 tablespoons
- Ground black pepper – 2 tablespoons

- Vegetable oil – 2 tablespoons
- Celery salt – 2 tablespoons
- Fresh chopped basil
- Honey jar – 1 (12 ounce)
- Wood chips – ½ pounds

Directions:

1. Get the grill preheated to high then soak the wood chips in water and place next to the grill.

2. Remove giblets and neck from turkey then rinse it and pat to dry. Next, place turkey into a disposable roasting pan.

3. In a bowl, combine ground black pepper, sage, basil, vegetable oil and salt. Pour the mixture over the turkey evenly then turn turkey breast side downwards on in the pan and loosely tent with aluminum foil.

4. Place the roasting pan over the preheated grill then add a handful of wood chips to the burning coals. Close the lid and allow to cook for about 1 hour.

5. Add more handfuls of soaked wood chips into the fire then drizzle honey over turkey and replace the foil. Close the lid of the grill again and allow it to cook for 2 more hours or

until the internal temperature of the thickest part reaches 180 deg. F.

6. Uncover turkey then turn the breast side up and baste with the remaining honey. Let the turkey stay uncovered for about 15 minutes.

7. Serve and enjoy

Smoked Chuck Roast

A great Sunday pot roast with an extra touch of smoked flavor.

Time: 10 Hours 10 Minutes

Serves: 6

Ingredients:

- Chuck roast – 4lbs
- White or yellow onion sliced – 1
- Beef Stock – 3 Cups

- Simple Beef Rub:
- Kosher salt – 2 tablespoons
- Coarse black pepper – 2 tablespoons
- Garlic powder – 2 tablespoons

Directions:

1. Set the smoker to 225 deg. F then get it preheated with the lid closed for 15 minutes.

2. In a small bowl combine all the ingredients for the rub, then rub onto the beef roast liberally using your hands to press the rub into the meat surface.

3. You can also rub the meat a night before smoking then refrigerate.

4. Place the roast directly over the grill grate with the fat side facing upwards. Cook for about 3 hours as you spray with a cup of beef stock. Reserve the remaining 2 cups of beef stock.

5. Once the three hours are up, turn up heat then place the sliced onions at the bottom of a disposable aluminum foil then pour the remaining beef stock at the bottom of the pan.

6. Transfer roast into the pan over the onions then set the pan to grill.

7. Increase the grill temperature to 250 deg. F then cook the roast until the internal temperature is 165 deg. F or for about 3 more hours.

8. Once the roast hits 165 deg. F, you can then tightly cover the pan using aluminum foil as you continue to cook until the instant-read meat thermometer reads 200 deg. F.

9. Get the pan out of the smoker and allow to rest for about 10 minutes. Remove roast from cooking liquid, next shred roast and remove fat from the cooking liquid.

10. Use the remaining liquid to moisten the roast.

11. Serve and enjoy.

Smoked Juicy Lamb Leg

Moist and juicy with a delicious crust on the outside.

Time: 4 Hours 10 Minutes

Serves: 6

Ingredients:

- Lamb leg deboned – 6lb
- One large onion
- Cloves of garlic – 4
- Cumin – 1 teaspoon
- Flat leaf parsley – 1 cup
- Kosher salt – 1 tablespoon

- Cumin – 1 teaspoon
- Camo seasoning – 3 tablespoons

Directions:

1. To make the marinade, combine garlic, cumin and onion then blend using a food processor into a fine paste.

2. Season the lamb on both sides with salt then place into a container. Slather onion paste over the meat on both sides then cover and allow to stay overnight in the fridge.

3. Fire up the smoker and allow it to cook at 250 deg. F then remove lamb from the marinade. Season lamb on the inner side with camo seasoning the place to roast into the smoker and cook for 3 hours or until an inserted thermometer reads 138 deg. F.

4. Once the lamb is cooked, wrap it in 2 layers using butcher's paper then place into a cooler and allow to rest for about 45 minutes.

5. Remove from the cooler then unwrap and slice to serve.

Beef Brisket Smoked

This is a great recipe for a perfect smoked brisket anytime. Very easy to prepare and delicious.

Time: 8 Hours 10 Minutes

Serves: 8

Ingredients:

- Beef brisket – 10 lbs.

Rub:

- Kosher salt – ½ cup
- Black pepper – ½ cup

Directions:

1. In a shallow bowl, mix black pepper and kosher salt

2. Shake a good amount of pepper and salt then rub it over the meat. Pat it over the surface of the meat as you ensure that the brisket is covered in every part.

3. Get the smoker preheated to 225 deg. F then add the wood chips.

4. Place the patted meat into the smoker. The fatty side should be facing up.

5. Have the meat smoked for 4 hours or until the internal temperature is 165 deg. F

6. Once the desired temperature is attained, remove meat from the smoker then wrap the brisket tightly to keep the cooking juices in.

7. Return brisket to the smoker then allow it to cook for another 4 hours or until the temperature of the meat gets to 205 deg. F.

8. Remove brisket from the smoker then allow to rest for about 30 minutes before slicing.

9. Slice, serve and enjoy.

Texas Smoked Beef Chuck

Prepared easier and faster than brisket. It is tender and moist and equally delicious as the traditional Texas brisket.

Time: 4 Hours 30 Minutes

Serves: 4

Ingredients:

- Beef chuck roast – 4 lbs.
- Texas rub – 2 tablespoons (blend 1/3-part kosher salt with 2/3 course ground pepper)

Directions:

1. Start charcoal for the smoker and allow it to produce ash before adding meat. Fill water pan if well equipped.

2. For the offset smoker, place aluminum pan into the smoking chamber then keep it filled with water.

3. Trim chuck roast of excess fat and discard then rub the salt and pepper blend over the chuck roast.

4. Smoke the roast with steady wisp of smoke for about 3 hours and leave the cover vent open fully during smoking.

5. After smoking for 2 hours, wrap the chuck in aluminum foil then place it back in the smoker.

6. Heat the oven to 300 deg. F then place the wrapped chuck on a baking sheet. Cook it for about 90 minutes as you occasionally check for tenderness.

7. When the meat begins to pull apart, remove from the oven then serve with preferred vegetables.

Smoky Grilled Vegetables

These crunchy vegetables can be used as a side to your steak or a scrumptious veggie sandwich.

Time: 55 Minutes

Serves: 4

Ingredients:

- Halved and seeded red bell peppers – 2
- Halved and seeded yellow bell peppers – 2
- Sliced zucchini – 2
- Sliced eggplant – 1 (sliced in small half rounds)
- Large onions sliced and peeled – 2

- Teriyaki sauce – 1 cup
- Vegetable oil – 4 tablespoons

Directions:

1. Brush the vegetables with vegetable oil to coat.

2. Prepare the smoker as per the manufacturer's instructions then place the veggies on the smoker rack in a single layer.

3. Smoke the vegetables for about 30 minutes.

4. Get the grill preheated over high heat. Brush the grate with oil then arrange the vegetables over the grill alongside peppers but away from the center.

5. Cook the vegetables for about 15 minutes as you turn once.

6. Baste the vegetables with teriyaki sauce while the vegetables cook, remove the tender pieces from the grill and continue to cook until all the vegetables are done.

Easy Smoked Turkey

Smoked turkey is the perfect choice for Thanksgiving or any other elegant occasion.

Time: 4 Hours 20 Minutes

Serves: 12

Ingredients:

- Whole turkey thawed – 12 pounds
- Chopped fresh savory – 1 tablespoon
- Ground black pepper – 1tablespoon

- Fresh sage chopped
- Olive oil – 1/8 cup
- Salt – 1 tablespoon
- Water – ½ cup

Directions:

1. Rinse the turkey then use paper towels to pat it dry. In a bowl combine savory, black pepper, salt and sage.

2. Rub half of the hub mixture inside the turkey then loosen the turkey's skin around the legs and breast and rub beneath the loosened skin with the remaining hub mixture.

3. Rub over the entire turkey with olive oil.

4. Place 20 lit charcoal briquettes on each side of the lower grate of the charcoal grill.

5. Place a drip pan in the middle of the lower grate then add in water. Add a piece of hickory or wood of your choice over the coals, once they are gray with ash.

6. Place turkey in the cooking grate then cover the grill and monitor the heat using a grill thermometer to maintain 250 deg. F.

7. You can add more wood if the pieces burn away to keep a steady flow of smoke.

8. Smoke turkey for about 20 minutes per each pound (4 hours) and increase heat to 250 deg. F in the last hour of smoking.

9. An instant read thermometer that's inserted at the thickest of the thigh should read 165 deg. F

10. Remove from the smoker then allow to cool for 15 minutes.

11. Serve and enjoy.

Ice and Fire Smoked Salmon

The fiery flavor of the red pepper flakes combined with the fresh mint taste makes a smoked salmon like no other.

Time:1 Hours 15 Minutes

Serves: 6

Ingredients:

- Salmon – 1 (4 pound)
- Fresh mint leaves finely chopped – ½ cup
- Crushed red pepper flakes – ½ cup

- Brandy to taste
- Brown sugar – ½ cup
- Salt – 2 tablespoons
- Alder wood chips – 2 cups

Directions:

1. Mix in a bowl brown sugar, crushed red pepper flakes, salt, mint leaves and brandy then make a paste.

2. Rub the mixture all over salmon then wrap using a plastic wrap and refrigerate overnight.

3. Get an outdoor grill preheated as you lightly oil the grate. Soak alder wood chips in water to begin smoking then turn the heat to lowest setting and position salmon over the grate as you close the lid.

4. Cook salmon for about 1 hour as you smoke it until it brings out a red brown color.

5. Remove from the smoker then allow to cool then serve and enjoy.

Texas Smoked Flounder

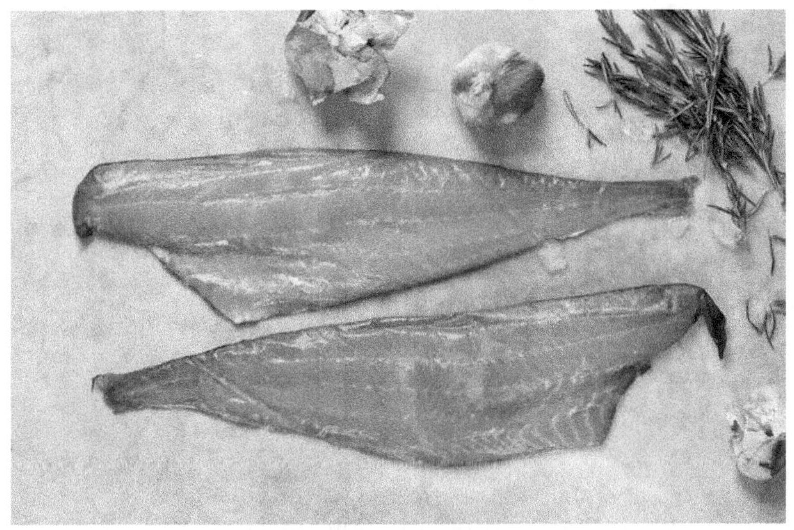

Texas Smoked Flounder, a great treat for any occasion.

Time: 45 Minutes

Serves: 2

Ingredients:

- Ground black pepper to taste
- Olive oil – 1 tablespoon
- Whole flounder – 1
- Halved lemon – 1
- Chopped fresh dill – 2 tablespoons

- Soaked wood chips

Directions:

1. Get the smoker preheated to high heat of about 350 deg. F. Scale and clean the flounder then make slits on the fish using a sharp knife.

2. Slice the half lemon into thinner slices then rub olive oil all over the fish as you squeeze lemon all over it.

3. Press a tablespoon of dill into the cut slits on the fish body then firmly insert the thinner lemon slices.

4. Place the fish over an aluminum foil then fold the sides high up around the fish. Foil should be sufficient to seal it into a package.

5. Place fish into the smoker then add in a few pieces of soaked wood chips over the coals.

6. Close the lid then thoroughly smoke the fish for about 10 minutes. Once the fish is flavored with the smoke, seal up the foil then move over direct heat as desired. You can still smoke it until completely done.

7. Once the fish is done, it should easily flake when using a fork.

8. Remove fish from the grill then garnish with the remaining fresh dill.

9. Serve and enjoy.

Smoked Pulled Pork

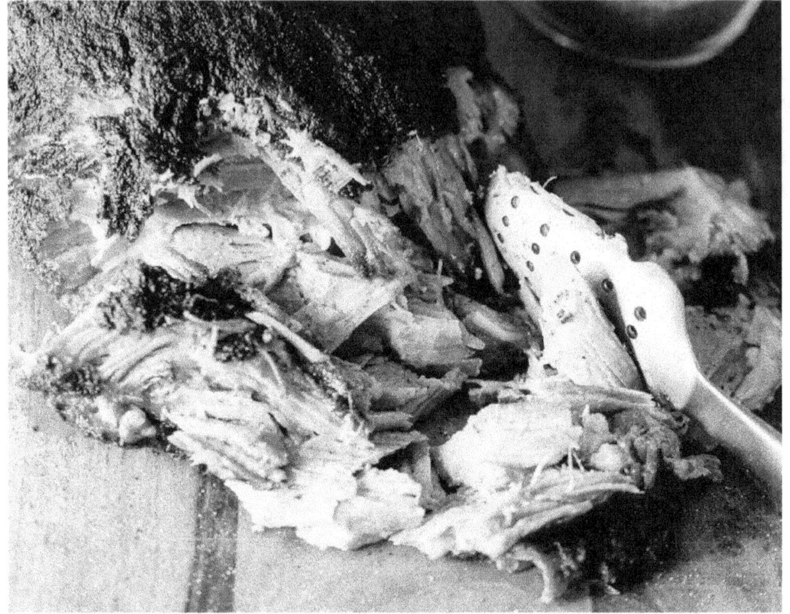

This easy to prepare Smoked Pulled Pork shoulder is marinated in a tasty blend of apple cider and spices then smoked until tender for a delicious dinner.

Time: 8 Hours 10 Minutes

Serves: 8

Ingredients:

- Pork shoulder roast – 8 pounds
- Apple cider – 1 quart

- Barbecue Rub:

- White and brown sugar – 5 tablespoons

- Paprika – 2 tablespoons

- Kosher salt – 2 tablespoons

- Freshly ground black pepper – 1 tablespoon

- Onion powder – 1 tablespoon

- Garlic powder – 1 tablespoon

- Hickory chips soaked in water – 2 cups

- Chopped onion – 1

Directions:

1. In a large pot place the pork shoulder then add apple cider and cover.

2. Combine both white and brown sugar together in a bowl then add paprika, salt, black pepper, onion powder and garlic powder, then mix well and add ¼ cup mixture of the sugar rub into the cider then reserve the remaining rub.

3. Cover the pot then place in the refrigerator and allow to stay for 12 hours. Prepare the smoker and set it to about 210 deg. F. Add wood stick to the smoker.

4. Pour cider brine into the smoker's water pan then add onion and ¼ cup of sugar rub. Spread the remaining rub over the pork shoulder, next transfer to the center of the smoker.

5. Smoke the pork for about 8 hours or until tender as you monitor the hickory chips and liquid while also adding more water as required.

6. Transfer pork into a large platter then allow to cool for about 30 minutes before you shred it using a fork.

Smoked Trout

The taste of this simple homemade Smoked Trout is incomparable and totally worth the effort.

Time: 2 hours and 30 minutes)

Serves: 4

Ingredients:

- Trout fillets – 2 pounds
- Olive oil – 2 tablespoons
- Crushed dried rosemary – 1 ½ tablespoons
- Curing mixture sugar based – 1 cup

- Ground black pepper to taste
- Chopped cloves garlic – 4
- Water – 1 quart

Directions:

1. Rinse the fillets the place them in a glass baking dish. Drizzle with olive oil then season with rosemary and garlic. Rub the seasonings right into the fish then cover the dish and refrigerate overnight.

2. Get the curing salt dissolved in the water then add into the dish with fish. Allow it to marinate for about 15 minutes per half inch of the thickness.

3. Prepare the smoker using charcoal then get the temperature to 150 deg. F before you get started. Get fish off the brine then discard the remaining liquid.

4. Place each piece of fish into aluminum foil then season with ground black pepper to taste.

5. Place the fish over the smoker rack then add some soaked wood chips over the coals. Cover it then allow to smoke for about 2 hours while you add wood chips as desired.

6. Increase the smoker heat to about 200 deg. F then allow the filet to smoke until the fillet's internal temperature gets to 165 deg. F.

7. Remove it from the smoker and allow to rest for about 20 minutes before serving.

Smoked Beef Ribs

A difference in barbecue choice. Cook this delicious Smoked Beef to tender perfection and wow your guests.

Time: 7 Hours 30 Minutes

Serves: 4

Ingredients:

- Whole beef ribs - 4lbs
- Jack Daniels beef rub – ¼ cup
- White vinegar – ¼ cup
- Jack Daniels – 2 tablespoons

Directions:

1. To prepare the smoker, use hardwood lump charcoal to light the fire then let it burn for about 15 minutes.

2. Season the beef ribs with Jack Daniels rub thoroughly.

3. Once the fire hits 300 deg. F add beef rib plate to the grill and some Western Barbecue pecan wood chips. Let it smoke for about 3 hours.

4. Once the 3 hours are up, add white vinegar and Jack Daniels whiskey to a bottle then use to spray the beef after every hour for about 3 more hours or until the internal temperature hits 205 deg. F.

5. Once the beef hits the desired internal temperature, pull off the grill then wrap in a tin with parchment paper. Place the beef ribs into an insulated cooler for 1 hour.

6. Pull the ribs out then slice and enjoy.

Cedar Planked Salmon

Grilling this tender flaky fish on cedar wood infuses a delicious flaky flavor.

Time: 1 Hour 40 Minutes

Serves: 4

Ingredients:

- Salmon fillets with skin removed – 2 pounds
- Fresh ginger root grated – 1 tablespoon

- Minced garlic – 1 teaspoon
- Chopped green onions – ¼ cup
- Sesame oil – 1 teaspoon
- Soy sauce – 1/3 cup
- Rice vinegar – 1 ½ cup
- Vegetable oil – 1/3 cup
- Untreated cedar planks – 3 (12inch)

Directions:

1. Get the cedar planks soaked in water for at least 1 hour.

2. In a bowl, add in vegetable oil, sesame oil, rice vinegar, green onions and soy sauce then mix well until combined.

3. Place salmon fillets into the marinade then turn to coat well. Cover and let it marinate for about 15 minutes.

4. Get the grill preheated to medium heat and place cedar planks on the grate.

5. Place salmon fillets over the planks as you discard the marinade. Cover the grill and let it cook for about 20 minutes.

6. Remove fish from the grill once ready, it will continue cooking even after being removed from the grill.

7. Once the fish is done it will easily flake when using a fork.

8. Serve and enjoy.

Smoked Lamb Leg

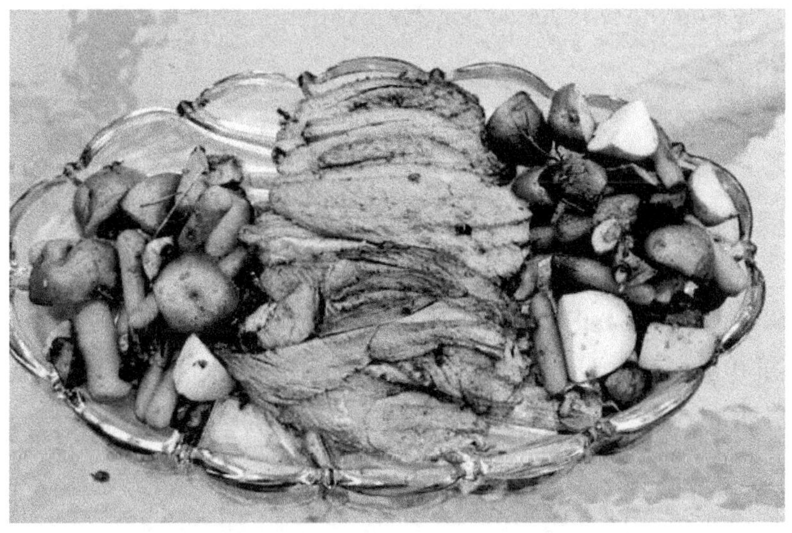

Enjoy this moist, juicy, Smoked Lamb Leg. A great main dish that's totally worth it.

Time: 3 Hours 10 Minutes

Serves: 6

Ingredients:

- Leg of lamb boneless – 3lb
- Ground black pepper – 2 tablespoons
- Dried oregano – 2 tablespoons
- Smoking wood chunks or chips of preference

Directions:

1. Set up the smoker as per the instructions then preheat it to 250 deg. F.

2. Use seasoning blend to liberally rub over all sides of the lamb, you can mix all the seasoning together.

3. Place the lamb over the grill directly with the fat side facing up. Replenish charcoal or the smoking wood then continue with the smoking process at 250 deg. F range.

4. Smoke the lamb until the internal temperature gets to 150 deg. F or until the desired doneness is attained.

5. Transfer lamb onto a cutting board then allow to rest for 10 minutes. You can tent it loosely with aluminum foil to keep it warm.

6. Carve then serve immediately.

Smoked Vegetables

The first thing that comes to mind when you hear the word 'smoked' is meat but try this Smoked Vegetables recipe and you will not regret it.

Time: 4 Hours 15 Minutes

Serves: 4

Ingredients:

- Sliced zucchini – 2 (cut into ¾ inch disks)
- Sliced yellow squash – 2 (cut into ¾ inch disks)
- Red onion medium (cut into wedges)

- Red pepper seeded – 1 (cut into strips)
- Small red potatoes – 6 (cut into small chunks)

Balsamic Vinaigrette:

- Olive oil – 1/3 cup
- Dijon mustard – 2
- Salt and pepper – 1 teaspoon
- Balsamic vinegar – ¼ cup

Directions:

1. To prepare the vinaigrette; combine all the ingredients in a bowl then whisk together until well blended.

2. Place all the vegetables into a casserole dish then pour the prepared balsamic vinaigrette and toss until the vegetables are well coated.

3. Place the dish with the vegetables over a smoker that's heated at 225 deg. F then smoke the vegetables for about 4 hours.

4. Remove from the smoker when ready then allow to cool for a few minutes.

5. Serve and enjoy.

Wagyu Beef Hot Dogs with Smashed Avocado

Fire up your grill and enjoy this great all beef hot dog with smashed Avocado.

Time 1 Hour

Serves: 3

Ingredients:

- 10 American Wagyu beef hot dogs
- Korobuta bacon (1.5-lbs, 0.7-kgs)
- Barbecue seasoning – 1 teaspoon

- 2 avocadoes
- Sea salt
- 10 brioche hot dog buns
- Cheddar cheese, shredded – ½ cup
- Preheat the smoker to 275°F (135°C)

Directions:

1. Wrap a piece of bacon around each hot dog and sprinkle all over with Barbecue seasoning and arrange on the preheated grill.

2. Cook the bacon wrapped sausages for just over 45 minutes until the bacon is thoroughly cooked.

3. In the meantime, peel and de-pit the avocadoes. Smash the flesh and season to taste with sea salt.

4. Spread the smashed avocado inside each hot dog buns and fill each with a cooked bacon wrapped sausage.

5. Sprinkle over the cheddar cheese and serve straight away.

Bacon-Wrapped Scotch Eggs

Perfect main course, appetizer or even a Keto snack. Try it, you will love it.

Time 1 Hour 15 Minutes

Serves: 6

Ingredients:

- Pork breakfast sausage meat (1-lb, 0.45-kgs)
- 6 slices of bacon
- 6 large eggs

- 1 egg, freshly beaten
- Breadcrumbs, as needed
- Barbecue sauce, store-bought, of choice

Directions

1. Preheat your electric smoker to 275°F (135°C)

2. Boil the eggs in a pan of boiling water for 5 minutes.

3. Allow the eggs to cook in an ice-filled bowl. Peel the eggs.

4. Divide the sausage meat into 6 equal portions. Wrap a portion of sausage meat around each egg.

5. Dip the sausage wrapped eggs first in the beaten egg and then roll in the breadcrumbs to evenly coat.

6. Wrap each egg in one slice of bacon. Repeat until all six eggs are prepared.

7. Arrange the eggs on the smoker and smoke for 45 minutes.

8. Brush each wrapped egg with barbecue sauce and smoke for an additional 15 minutes.

9. Serve.

Smoked Top Sirloin Roast

Roast it low and slow for that juicy smoked flavor.

Time: 3 Hours 10 Minutes

Serves: 8

Ingredients:

- Top sirloin beef roast – 6lbs
- Montreal steak spice – ¼ cup
- Sea salt – 3 tablespoons

Directions:

1. Trim any excess fat from the roast. If desired, you can tie up the roast with kitchen twine.

2. Rub the roast with sea salt all the way through then rub it again with Montreal steak spice.

3. Set the smoker up for 250 deg. F using wood of choice.

4. Lay the roast on the smoker rack and let it smoke for three hours or until the desired doneness is attained.

5. Remove from the smoker then allow to stay for 10 minutes.

6. Slice, serve and enjoy.

Texan Beef Brisket

An ebony colored crust with a tender, mouthwatering, juicy, smoked flesh underneath.

Time 16 Hours 30 Minutes

Serves: 18

Ingredients:

- 1 whole packer brisket, chilled (12-lbs, 5.5-kgs)
- Garlic powder – 2 tablespoons
- Salt – 2 tablespoons
- Black pepper – 2 tablespoons

Directions:

1. Preheat smoker to 225°f (107°c) using hardwood smoke and indirect heat.

2. Arrange the brisket so the point end is underneath. Cut away and discard any excess fat.

3. Trim down the crescent-shaped fat section to ensure a smooth transition between point and flat. Trim any excess fat from the point. Square the ends and edges of the flat.

4. Flip the brisket and trim the fat cap down to a ¼-ins (0.6-cms) thick.

5. In a small bowl, combine the garlic, salt, and pepper. Sprinkle the mixture over the whole brisket.

6. Arrange the brisket in the smoker with the point end facing the heat source. Close the lid and cook for approximately 8 hours until the internal temperature registers 165°f (73°c).

7. Roll out a piece of butcher paper and arrange the brisket in the center. Wrap the paper around the brisket securely so that it is leak-proof. Return the parcel to the smoker and arrange seam side down. Close the smoker lid and continue

to cook until the internal temperature registers 200°f (93°c). This will take approximately 6-7 hours.

8. Allow the cooked meat to rest for an hour before slicing and serving against the grain.

New York Strip Steak with Bourbon Butter

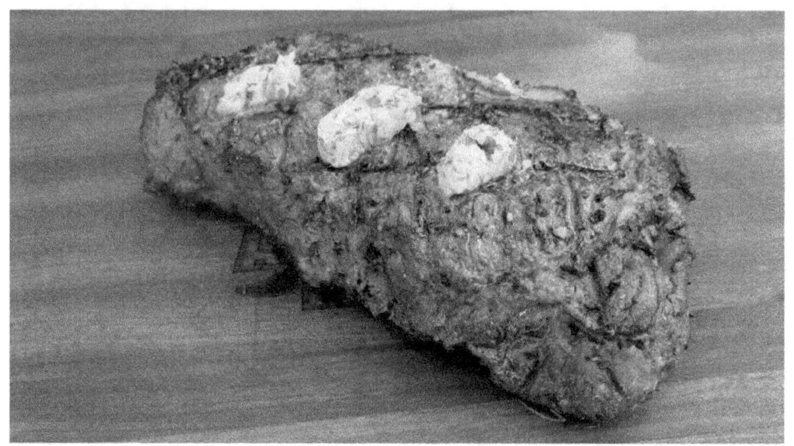

An awesome dinner choice; will have your guests asking for seconds.

Time 1 Hour 30 Minutes

Serves: 2

Ingredients:

- 2 New York strip steaks
- Salted butter, room temperature – ½ cup
- Fresh parsley, chopped – 1 tablespoon
- 1 green onion top, minced
- Bourbon – 2 tablespoons

- Smoked paprika – 1 teaspoon
- Steak rub

Directions

1. Preheat smoker to 225°f (107°c) using pecan wood chips

2. First, prepare the butter. Combine the butter, parsley, green onion, bourbon, and paprika in a small bowl. Transfer to plastic wrap, shape into a log and roll tightly. Chill until ready to use.

3. Season the steaks with steak rub and place in the smoker. Cook for approximately 60 minutes until the internal temperature registers 130°f (55°c), for medium-rare.

4. Place a skillet over high heat. When the steak is cooked to your liking, sear each piece on both sides in the skillet.

5. Top with a couple slices of bourbon butter and serve straight away.

Cheddar and Onion Pig Shots

An interesting, tasty appetizer, smoked pig shots with cheddar cheese and onions.

Time 2 Hours

Serves: 20

Ingredients:

The Meat:

- 10 thickly slices of bacon, cut in half (1-lb, 0.45-kgs)
- 1 smoked sausage link, cut into 20 pieces

The Filling:

- Cream cheese (8-ozs, 0.23-kgs)
- Pork rub, of choice – 3 tablespoons
- 1 block Cheddar cheese, cut into (0.5–ins, 1.25-cms) cubes
- ¼ onion, peeled and diced
- Onions, diced – 10 teaspoons

Directions:

1. Preheat your electric smoker for indirect cooking to 250°F (121°C)

2. Fill the water pan with water

3. Apple wood chips are recommended for this recipe

4. First, prepare the cream cheese filling. Add the cream cheese to a bowl along with 3 tablespoons of your favorite rub and mix to combine.

5. Transfer the mixture to a large zip lock bag. Snip the corner of the bag to form a piping bag.

6. Wrap half a slice of bacon around each piece of sausage and using a toothpick, seal.

7. Repeat the process until you have made 20 pig shots in total.

8. Fill the shots with Cheddar cheese, cream cheese rub mixture, and diced onion.

9. Arrange a Cheddar cheese cube on top of each shot.

10. Using the piping bag, fill the shots with the remaining cream cheese rub filling.

11. Garnish with a ½ teaspoon of diced onions.

12. Sprinkle with more of the rub.

13. Arrange the pig shots on a tray and place in the smoker.

14. Smoke for 90 minutes, until the meat is cooked, and the cheese is entirely melted.

Herb-Stuffed Pork Chops

Herb-Stuffed Pork Chops seasoned to the bone and a rich smoked flavor.

Time 1 Hour 15 Minutes

Serves: 4

Ingredients:

- 4 thick cut 1-ins (2.5-cms) thick pork loin chops
- Herb seasoned stuffing, store-bought – 2 cups
- Salt and black pepper

Directions:

1. Preheat to 325°F (163°C) with the lid closed, for 10-15 minutes

2. First, prepare the pork chops by cutting a deep pocket into the side of each one using a sharp knife. Cut towards the bone, while taking care not to cut all the way through.

3. Prepare the store-bought stuffing mix according to the package instructions.

4. Generously stuff each chop pocket with the stuffing mixture and season with salt and black pepper.

5. Lay the pork chops directly on the grill grate and cook for between 45-50 minutes, until the pork registers an internal temperature of 160°F (71°C). You will not need to flip the chops over during cooking.

6. Allow the pork to rest for a few minutes before transferring to a serving platter.

7. Serve.

Conclusion

You will notice from these recipes; the smoking world can be exciting as you want it to be and not limited to your imagination. You can smoke just about anything – meat, vegetable, mineral, savory, sweet!

As you acquaint yourself with these recipes, don't hesitate to get started on your own. The basic principles stand but let your taste buds drive you.

Happy smoking, enjoy!